S0-AHU-072

Livonia Public Library
ALFRED NOBLE BRANCH
32901 PLYMOUTH ROAD
Livonia, Michigan 48150-1793
(734)421-6600
LIVN #19

J973.311
D

19

KALEIDOSCOPE

THE BOSTON TEA PARTY

by

Edward F. Dolan

BENCHMARK BOOKS

MARSHALL CAVENDISH
NEW YORK

Livonia Public Library
ALFRED NOBLE BRANCH
32901 PLYMOUTH ROAD
Livonia, Michigan 48150-1793
(734)421-6600
LIVN #19

Benchmark Books
Marshall Cavendish Corporation
99 White Plains Road
Tarrytown, NY 1059
Website: www.marshallcavendish.com

Copyright © 2002 by Marshall Cavendish Corporation
All rights reserved.

Library of Congress Cataloging-in-Publication Data
Dolan, Edward F., date
The Boston Tea Party / by Edward F. Dolan.
    p.cm. – (Kaleidoscope)
Includes bibliographical references and index.
ISBN 0-7614-1303-0
1. Boston Tea Party, 1773—Juvenile literature. [1. Boston Tea Party, 1773.] I. Title. II. Kaleidoscope (Tarrytown, N.Y.)
E215.7 .D65 2001   973.3'115—dc21   00-049801

Photo Research by Anne Burns Images

Cover Photo: North Wind Pictures

The photographs in this book are used by permission and through the courtesy of:
Photo researchers/ Northwind Picture Archives: 5, 7, 18, 22, 24, 29, 33, 37, 38, 41.
The Bridgeman Art Library: 14, 21, 43. The Granger Collection: 9, 11, 17, 27, 30, 35.
Corbis/Bettman: 13.

Printed in Italy

6 5 4 3 2 1

MAR 1 4 2002

3 9082 08595 7457

CONTENTS

A NIGHT IN HISTORY

On the night of December 16, 1773, three British merchant ships lay alongside Griffin's Wharf in the city of Boston. They carried cargoes of tea packed in wooden cases.

Rain had fallen throughout the day. But now the sky was clear and crowded with stars. Suddenly, the sparkle of the stars was joined by the yellow glow of lanterns swinging along the wharf. Holding the lanterns high were some 150 strangely dressed marchers. Blankets hung from their shoulders. Single feathers crowned their heads. They carried axes and hatchets.

This seems to be an Indian attack. But these men are really Boston colonists in disguise. They are giving early American history one of its most memorable nights—the night of the Boston Tea Party.

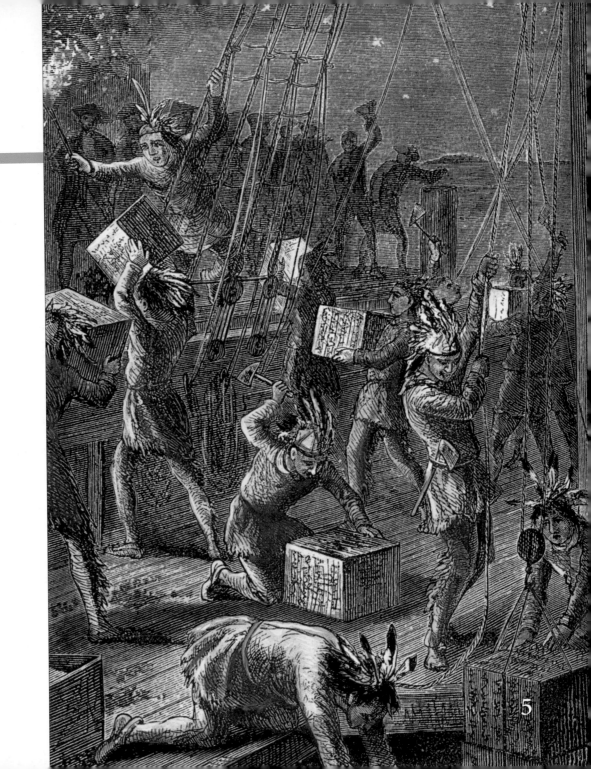

5

In the lanterns' light, they could have been easily mistaken for Indians. But they were really men of Britain's Massachusetts Colony. They had disguised themselves for the night's work ahead. Their outfits were meant to keep their identities a secret from the Boston authorities, who would be infuriated by what was going to happen and would surely want to take revenge for it.

Behind the disguised men hurried a crowd of people out to watch the coming adventure—an adventure that would be remembered for centuries as the Boston Tea Party.

Boston citizens of all ages watch and cheer from the docks as the "Indians" dump the shipments of hated British tea into the waters of the harbor.

YEARS OF TROUBLE

The Boston Tea Party was the result of years of growing trouble between Britain's King George III and his American colonies. Much of the conflict sprang from the taxes that he and his Parliament demanded of the colonists.

One of the most hated taxes of all was contained in a law passed in 1767. It was a tariff (a special tax) that the Americans had to pay when buying various goods shipped from England. Chief among these goods was tea.

The tariff angered Americans everywhere because tea was their favorite beverage. They bought tons of it every year. The tax would cost them dearly.

King George III of Great Britain.

9

Also, the tariff was of a special nature. Most taxes were charged to business firms. But this one was charged to the people. To the Americans, this was an outrage. The king had no right to tax them directly! They were not even represented in Parliament. No one spoke for them when laws were being passed.

Their anger triggered riots in a number of towns. The outbreaks so alarmed Parliament that it changed the tariff law to calm the people. It lowered the tax on tea and dropped all the others.

Actually, the tea tax had done far more than trigger rioting. It had caused many colonists to stop buying tea from Britain. Instead, they bought tea smuggled in from the West Indies.

The taxes King George imposed on the Americans triggered rioting throughout the colonies. Here, angry New Yorkers burn some official papers concerning the taxes.

Then, when the tax was lowered, they went on buying the smuggled tea. The result was havoc for the British tea merchants. More than seventeen million pounds of leaves were soon gathering dust in London warehouses. It would be a financial disaster if the tea went unsold.

But King George suddenly thought of a way to avoid such a disaster and end the American ban on tea at the same time. He decided to sell the leaves to the colonists at half price, plus a small tax. They would then be buying British tea for far less than smuggled tea. Surely, they would jump at this bargain.

He was dead wrong.

In another burst of anger, the people of New York pull down a statue of King George in this 1857 painting by William Walcott.

13

A PROMISE TO RESIST

The Americans felt nothing but insult. How could the king think that a lower price would make them forget the unfair tariff? They promised to resist the landing of any tea that now arrived from England.

Their promise was put to a test in late 1773. They learned that several British tea ships were sailing west and would arrive at the end of November. Some would land at New York City. Others would make port in Philadelphia, Pennsylvania, and Charleston, South Carolina. Three—the Dartmouth, Eleanor, and Beaver—were bound for Boston.

Britain's King George III is so unpopular with American colonists that he is often the subject of unflattering caricatures. In this cartoon by James Gillray, King George and Queen Charlotte enjoy a frugal meal.

15

A group of political leaders in Boston went to work as soon as the three ships docked at Griffin's Wharf. The group spent the next weeks asking the ship owners to sail their vessels, fully loaded, back to England. They also went to Thomas Hutchinson, the governor of Massachusetts, with the same request. All their pleas were turned down.

Popular hatred of Thomas Hutchinson, the last Royal Governor of Massachusetts Colony, is expressed in this 1774 cartoon.

Finally, December 16 arrived. The group assembled at a meeting hall to make a last effort to have the ships sent home. Some seven thousand people gathered in and around the building to watch a messenger carry the final appeal to Governor Hutchinson. Then they waited throughout the rainy afternoon for his reply.

The colonists demonstrate against the tea tax in the days just before the Tea Party. The sign reads "England's Folly and America's Ruin."

One of the group leaders was a local politician named Samuel Adams. He waited for Hutchinson's answer with a secret smile. He hoped that it would be a refusal. A refusal would enable him to carry out a plan that he had been working on for the entire month.

The governor's reply arrived just before six o'clock that evening. It was exactly what Adams had hoped for. He announced to the people in the hall that the ships would not be sent home.

Samuel Adams talks with his fellow Boston leaders a few hours before the Tea Party.

HERE FORMERLY STOOD
GRIFFINS WHARF,
AT WHICH LAY MOORED ON DEC. 16, 1773, THREE BRITISH SHIPS WITH CARGOES OF TEA.
TO DEFEAT KING GEORGE'S TRIVIAL BUT TYRANNICAL TAX OF THREE PENCE A POUND,
ABOUT NINETY CITIZENS OF BOSTON, PARTLY DISGUISED AS INDIANS, BOARDED THE SHIPS,
THREW THE CARGOES, THREE HUNDRED AND FORTY TWO CHESTS IN ALL, INTO THE SEA,
AND MADE THE WORLD RING WITH THE PATRIOTIC EXPLOIT OF THE

BOSTON TEA PARTY
"NO! NE'ER WAS MINGLED SUCH A DRAUGHT
IN PALACE, HALL, OR ARBOR,
AS FREEMEN BREWED AND TYRANTS QUAFFED
THAT NIGHT IN BOSTON HARBOR."

Suddenly, there was a shrill whistle somewhere in the watching crowd. This was the signal to put his plan into action. A band of whooping Indians, brandishing axes and hatchets, burst into the hall. For a moment, the crowd was stunned. Were they under attack? Then there was laughter. The people could see that the seeming Indians were really their fellow Bostonians with chimney soot darkening their faces and blankets draped over their shoulders.

Voices joined the laughter as the Indians shouted: "Boston harbor a teapot tonight! To Griffin's Wharf!"

The men dressed as Indians streamed out the front door. The people, both inside and outside the hall, began to follow them through the streets. Adams saw that they understood what was about to happen at Griffin's Wharf.

The Boston Tea Party was underway.

This plaque is a memorial to the Boston Tea Party. It can be found today at Griffin's Wharf, Boston.

OVERBOARD AND INTO THE WATER

Some fifty so-called Indians departed the hall. They were joined by about one hundred others as they marched through the streets. The newcomers had put on their costumes at home or at the houses of friends.

When the Indians reached Griffin's Wharf, they divided themselves into three bands of about fifty men each. Each band had a leader and was assigned to a ship. Two bands boarded the Dartmouth and Eleanor, which were berthed at dockside. The Beaver lay a few yards offshore and had to be pulled over to the dock by the ship's mooring ropes.

A replica of the tea
ship Beaver lies at
anchor alongside a
Boston dock.

Boston citizens watch in silence and then begin to cheer as the "Indians" haul the tea crates up into the night from the holds of the ships, break them open with axes, and then dump their contents overboard.

Once on board the ships, the leaders called for the first mates and politely asked for the keys to the holds. They explained that they had orders not to damage the ships and did not want their men breaking into the holds with their hatchets and axes. The keys were quietly handed over.

Then the night's work began. On each ship, ropes and pulleys were swung into position. The wooden cases were pulled to the deck and dropped at the rail. Their tops were split open as axes flashed in the lantern light. Finally, the boxes were lifted to the rail and tilted. The crowd on the dock watched in silence as streams of tea leaves poured into the harbor water, followed a moment later by the cases themselves.

27

Along with being told not to harm the ships, the attackers were under orders not to take any of the tea for themselves. However, a man named Charles O'Connor began stuffing handfuls of leaves into his coat while handling several cases. When someone saw him do his, he made a dash for the dock. But he was caught and stripped of his coat. Then, with a sharp kick, he was sent on his way.

Charles O'Connor's coat is put on display the day after the Tea Party.

The Boston Tea Party lasts only four hours. Case after case of tea is poured into the harbor in that time. Then the "Indians" sweep the decks and holds clean and leave the ships as they found them.

When all the cases were thrown overboard, the men swept the decks clean of any tea that had been accidentally spilled. Wooden strips from the cases were tossed into the water. Ropes and pulleys were properly stored. Then the first mates were called so they could see that everything was again shipshape.

Each ship carried more than one hundred cases of tea. In all, 342 cases had been emptied into the harbor. The Indians went down to the dock, shouldered their axes and hatchets—their "tomahawks" —and marched away. It was now ten o'clock. The Boston Tea Party had lasted only four hours.

AN INSPIRATION FOR OTHERS

The Boston Tea Party inspired other cities to oppose the un-wanted shipments. The people of Philadelphia and New York refused to accept their ship-ments and the ships returned to England. At Charlestown, the tea was eventually unloaded but it went into a storehouse.

Seen here are the tea ships anchored at Charleston, South Carolina. Their cargo will be removed and placed in a storehouse.

The Tea Party also marked a change in the attitude of the American colonists toward the crown. There had often been trouble between the two, but it had never made the colonists want to break free and start a country of their own. All they had wanted was the freedom to conduct the business of their colonies.

Following the Boston Tea Party, the American colonists begin to see that they need to break free of Great Britain and found a nation of their own. The changing American view causes heated debates in town meetings everywhere.

Many colonists remained loyal to Britain. But their numbers were soon matched by those made furious by the steps that the king and Parliament took in revenge for the Tea Party. In 1774 five laws were passed that the Americans called the Intolerable Acts. Among the Intolerable Acts were laws requiring that:

• The port of Boston be closed until the people paid for the destroyed tea.

British warships lie at anchor in Boston harbor during the weeks following the Tea Party. They are enforcing a British ruling that the port be closed until the Americans pay for the destroyed tea.

STON WITH SEVERAL SHIPS OF WAR IN THE HARBOU

• The officials of Massachusetts no longer be elected but named by the king.

• The governor be permitted to house British troops in public and private buildings. (This was an old, hated law that Britain had discarded.)

The Tea Party leads to the new use of an old and dated British law. The Americans are once again required to house British troops in their homes and public buildings.

Though the Intolerable Acts were aimed mainly at Massachusetts, they angered Americans everywhere. As a result, the colonies sent delegates to a Philadelphia conference that went down in American history as the First Continental Congress. The delegates aired their complaints against British rule and sent a Declaration of Colonial Rights and Grievances to King George. In the declaration, they politely asked him to right the wrongs being done to the colonies and reminded him that they were still loyal to England. Despite their reminders, the king angrily ignored their request.

Throughout the colonies, the Americans clash with the British soldiers who are sent to enforce the Intolerable Acts.

King George stubbornly ignores the request of the Americans to right the wrongs being done to them. His silence leads to the writing of the Declaration of Independence and the day that it is read aloud throughout the colonies.

In ignoring the request, George drove a deeper wedge between the Mother Country and its American colonies. The Revolutionary War and the independence it would bring became more than a dream to an ever-growing number of colonists. In 1775, armed rebellion became a reality.

TIMELINE

1767 The British government imposes a special tax on American colonists to pay for tea and other goods.

The colonists stop buying British tea. Instead they purchase tea smuggled from the West Indies.

1773 Several tea ships sail from England, bound for four American cities, among them Boston.

Colonists disguised as Indians invade Griffith's Wharf and head for the docked ships. They dump cases of tea overboard.

1774 The British government takes revenge for the Boston Tea Party by passing the Intolerable Acts.

Colonial leaders respond by holding what becomes known as the First Continental Congress.

1775 The American Revolutionary War erupts with fighting in Massachusetts, at Lexington and Concord.

FIND OUT MORE

BOOKS:

Alderman, Clifford Lindsey. *Samuel Adams: Son of Liberty.* New York: Holt, Rinehart and Winston, 1961.

Fradin, Dennis Brindell. *Samuel Adams: The Father of American Independence.* New York: Clarion Books, 1998.

Hall-Quint, Olga W. *Guardians of Liberty: Sam Adams and John Hancock.* New York: E.P. Dutton, 1976.

Langguth, A.J. Patriots: *The Men Who Started the American Revolution.* New York: Simon & Schuster, 1988.

Phelan, Mary. *The Story of the Boston Tea Party.* New York: Thomas Crowell, 1973.

WEBSITES:

Liberty! Chronicle of the Revolution: The Boston Tea Party.
http://www.pbs.org.ktca/liberty/chronicle/bostonteaparty-edenton.html

Kidport Reference Library

The Boston Tea Party
http://www.kidport.com/RefLib/UsaHistory/AmericanRevolution/TeaParty.htm

AUTHOR'S BIO

Edward F. Dolan is the author of over one hundred nonfiction books for young people and adults. He has written on medicine and science, law, history, folklore, and current social issues. Mr. Dolan is a native Californian, born in the San Francisco region and raised in Southern California. In addition to writing books, he has been a newspaper reporter and a magazine editor. He currently lives in the northern part of the state.

INDEX

Page numbers for illustrations are in boldface.